CELEBRATING THE NAME AMY

Celebrating the Name Amy

Walter the Educator

Silent King Books

Copyright © 2024 by Walter the Educator

All rights reserved. No part of this book may be reproduced in any manner whatsoever without written permission except in the case of brief quotations embodied in critical articles and reviews.

First Printing, 2024

Disclaimer
This book is a literary work; poems are not about specific persons, locations, situations, and/or circumstances unless mentioned in a historical context. This book is for entertainment and informational purposes only. The author and publisher offer this information without warranties expressed or implied. No matter the grounds, neither the author nor the publisher will be accountable for any losses, injuries, or other damages caused by the reader's use of this book. The use of this book acknowledges an understanding and acceptance of this disclaimer.

dedicated to everyone with the first name of Amy

AMY

Thought where dreams take flight,

AMY

There dwells a name of purest light,

AMY

Amy, a melody in the symphony of life,

AMY

A beacon amidst the tumult and strife.

AMY

In whispered winds and silent streams,

AMY

Her name echoes through ethereal beams,

AMY

A tapestry woven with threads divine,

AMY

Amy, the essence of a celestial design.

AMY

In gardens where the roses bloom,

AMY

Her name dances amid the sweet perfume,

AMY

Each petal adorned with grace untold,

AMY

Amy, a masterpiece of stories yet unfold.

AMY

In the depths of oceans where secrets lie,

AMY

Her name whispers beneath the azure sky,

AMY

A siren's call that stirs the soul,

AMY

Amy, a melody that makes the heart whole.

AMY

In the labyrinth of time's embrace,

AMY

Her name weaves through every space,

AMY

A compass guiding lost souls home,

AMY

Amy, a sanctuary where wanderers roam.

AMY

In the silence of the midnight hour,

AMY

Her name ignites a dormant power,

AMY

A phoenix rising from ashes of despair,

AMY

Amy, a flame that banishes every snare.

AMY

In the whispers of ancient lore,

AMY

Her name is etched forevermore,

AMY

A legacy written in stars above,

AMY

Amy, the embodiment of eternal love.

AMY

In the heart's deepest sanctuary,

AMY

Her name resonates with boundless clarity,

AMY

A symphony of hope in a world of fear,

AMY

Amy, a testament that destiny holds dear.

AMY

In the dance of shadows and light,

AMY

Her name paints the canvas of night,

AMY

A constellation guiding souls to soar,

AMY

Amy, a beacon shining evermore.

AMY

In the chronicles of history's tome,

AMY

Her name echoes through kingdoms and throne,

AMY

A timeless anthem sung by bards of old,

AMY

Amy, a tale of valor yet untold.

AMY

In the laughter of children at play,

AMY

Her name sparkles like sunbeams at bay,

AMY

A melody that lingers in the air,

AMY

Amy, a promise of joy beyond compare.

AMY

ABOUT THE CREATOR

Walter the Educator is one of the pseudonyms for Walter Anderson. Formally educated in Chemistry, Business, and Education, he is an educator, an author, a diverse entrepreneur, and he is the son of a disabled war veteran. "Walter the Educator" shares his time between educating and creating. He holds interests and owns several creative projects that entertain, enlighten, enhance, and educate, hoping to inspire and motivate you.

Follow, find new works, and stay up to date
with Walter the Educator™
at WaltertheEducator.com

www.ingramcontent.com/pod-product-compliance
Lightning Source LLC
LaVergne TN
LVHW021239080526
838199LV00088B/5200